doll School

For Girls Who Love to Teach!

⭐ American Girl®

Published by American Girl Publishing, Inc.

Questions or comments? Call 1-800-845-0005, visit our Web site at **americangirl.com**,
or write to Customer Service, American Girl, 8400 Fairway Place, Middleton, WI
53562-0497.

Printed in China
09 10 11 12 13 14 15 LEO 10 9 8 7 6 5 4 3

Editorial Development: Trula Magruder

Art Direction & Design: Camela Decaire

Production: Jeannette Bailey, Sarah Boecher, Judith Lary, Kendra Schluter

Photography: Studio R Photography

Illustrations: Casey Lukatz

Stylists: Camela Decaire, Carrie Anton, Mandy Crary

Dear Doll Lover,

Start a school for your dolls! Use the supplies and ideas in this kit to teach math, music, and more. Plan lessons. Explain information. Create tests. Grade papers. Reward your students. But don't stop there. Use what you've learned in school to create more tests and assignments.

Set up the classroom in a small area—a corner, a closet, or a patio.

And don't forget the routines. Hold tornado and fire drills, create bulletin boards, and design seating charts. If you'd like, invite a friend over to substitute teach, coach a sport, or give after-school lessons. There's the bell!

Your friends at American Girl

Set Up Class

Pull your classroom together with these tools.

Alphabet Banner

Pull out the alphabet banner and tape it around your classroom so that students can see the cursive letters when writing.

Desks & Decor

If you don't have doll desks, use boxes and pillows or doll-sized tables and chairs. Give yourself a desk, too. To pull the classroom area together, lay down a small rug, bath mat, or colorful towel.

In/Out Boxes

To organize school papers, decorate craft-box lids with pretty papers and ribbons. Pull out the stickers to label the lids. To stack lids, glue small wooden blocks on the back edge of the bottom lid. Squeeze glue on the top of each block, line up the back edge of the top lid, and then press it down onto the blocks. Let dry. Place the in/out boxes on your desk.

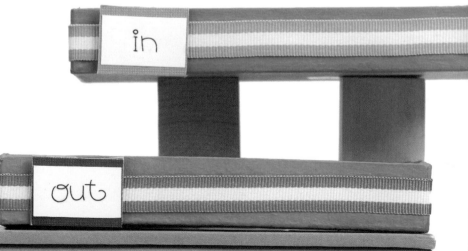

Bb Cc Dd Ee Ff Gg

Chalkboard & Whiteboard

Pull out the chalkboard for spelling practice, to show math problems, and to write your name. Write on the board with chalk and erase with a soft cloth or eraser.

Flip the chalkboard over for a whiteboard. Use it to advertise the day's lunch menu or add color to lectures. Write on the board with dry-erase markers only—never permanent ones. Clean the board with an eraser, paper towel, or cloth.

Easel

Display your students' artwork, homework assignments, school projects, and more on your class easel. Pull out the easel and prop it open.

Get Teacher's Tools

Stay organized with these supplies.

Attendance & Grade Book

Skip the stress at report-card time with an organized record. Pull out the "Teacher's Attendance & Grade Book" cover, the attendance sheet, and the grade sheet. Slip the sheets inside the cover and staple them together on the fold.

To track attendance, write each student's name on the attendance sheet. If a student is absent, mark that day's square with a slash. If that absence is excused, turn the slash into an X.

Write each student's name on the grade sheet also. To mark a grade, follow the assignment at the top and the student's name on the left until you find the intersecting square to enter the grade. Add your own assignments to the blanks.

Grading Folders

Stay on top of homework and exams with file folders. Fold each folder as shown below. To label folders, pull out the "To Be Graded" and the "Graded" stickers.

Grading Pencil

To make sure your writing stands out on student papers, use a different lead color—many teachers like red. Pull out the paper apple topper and slip it over your pencil for more pizzazz!

Report Cards

When it's report-card time, pull out the cards and assign one to each student. (If you have more than four students, photocopy the cover and sheet.) Before marking grades, review attendance and assignment grades.

Award Certificates

Pull out the certificates to give your students the recognition they deserve. Write a student's name on a certificate. Make sure that each student receives at least one award during the year.

Hall Passes

Fill out a hall pass any time a student needs to leave class.

School Locker

Assign each student a locker to organize her class work and books.

Locker

Give each student her very own school locker to store books, assignments, and personal gear. To make one, pull out the locker door sticker and press it to a shoe box lid. Attach one side of the lid to the shoe box. Use a clear, heavy-duty tape on the inside.

Locker Decorations

Help make each locker unique by decorating it. Hang up mini posters, cut out small photos from old magazines, or use mini sticky notes with messages.

Geography

Teach your students about the world they live in.

World Map

Familiarize students with the continents and oceans using a world map. Pull out the map, and then help your students color it in. Use a star sticker to mark where they are in the world.

Basketball Practice Wednesday 5 p.m.

Today's Lunch Menu
Hamburger
Green Beans
Milk

CONTIN
And Other Geo

MAP KEY

Mountains (Brown or green)

River (blue)

Latitude

Longitude

Antarctica is located at the **South Pole**. It
flat map along with the rest of the continent
an **inset**, like this, as if you were looking at

Science

Show your students a special view of nature.

Butterfly Exhibit

Explore the differences in *lepidoptera* with a butterfly exhibit. To make one, peel off the butterfly stickers, and place each one on the correct spot on the board.

Magnifying Glass

Reveal tiny details of your insects with a magnifying glass. To make it, punch out the frame.

Black Swallowtail

Green Swallowtail

Painted Lady

Gulf Fritillary

Peacock

Monarch

Vanessa Atalanta

Blue Morpho

Common Tiger

Language Arts

Drill students on how to read, write, and listen.

Mini Journals

Ask students to keep journals to track writing practice. Pull out the cover and pages, slip the pages inside the cover, and then staple them at the fold. If you have more than four students, photocopy the cover and pages.

Story Starters

Before class, write a short story using the story starters. Read the story to the class, and then assign a starter to each student.

Story Starters
for Writing Class

Clara the Cat didn't like goldfish or mice. She didn't like cat food much, either. In fact, what Clara did like to eat shock everyone—e Clara!

Amber loved b bees. She took

Writing Journal

Belongs to:

Social Studies

Promote the past with specialized history books.

Historical Fiction

Involve the class in history by reading a story about a girl from the 1910s. If you like, create a quiz or a project about the story.

MEET Rebecca

Spelling

Coach your class on the value of super spelling skills.

Spelling Quizzes

Pull out the quizzes and grade them. How well are your students absorbing their spelling lists? Give refresher lessons if they need some. Don't forget to enter spelling grades in the grade book. Give a gold star to a student who earns 90 or 100 percent. If you have more than four students, photocopy the tests.

CLARE
Student's N

Tea

Sarah S.
Student's Name

80 B

Unit 1/Spelling

Each

1. recess
2. holiday
   voice
   sh
5.
6. dance
7. taught
8. pancak
9. strawbe

1. reṡess ~~X~~ (c)
2. holiday
3. voice
4. jelyfish ~~X~~
   rainstorm
7. taught
8. pancake
9. strawberry

11. wrist
12. design
13. popcorn
14. square
15. volleyball
16. choklate ~~X~~ (co)
17. pretty
18. scream
19. drama

Handwriting

Instruct your pupils that practice makes perfect.

Handwriting Sheets

As you know, good cursive writing takes lots of practice. Pull out the practice sheets and hand them out daily. If you have more than four students or if you want to assign extra practice, photocopy the sheets.

My favorite flower is a daisy.

My favorite flower is a daisy.

My favorite flower is a daisy.

My favorite flower is a daisy.

My favorite flower is a daisy.

Arithmetic

Demonstrate to your class how much math matters.

Flash Cards

Students can work by themselves with flash cards. Pull out the multiplication deck for memorization practice.

Pocket Calculator

Keep a calculator handy for quick work. To make one, pull out the calculator sticker and press it onto a piece of cardboard. Cut around the sticker.

Emily
Student's Name

MATH: Unit 1
Multiplication

✗ 7 X 9 = 81   3. 7 X 5 = 35
2. 8 X 6 = 48   4. 9 X 8 = 72
5. 2 X 5 X 2 = 20   7. 1 X 9 X 2 = 18
✗ 3 X 5 X 2 = 16   ✗ 4 X 4 X 1 = 4

Show your work.

9. Ella made 3 daisy crowns. Each crown had 22 flowers. How many daisies did Ella pick?

22
X 3
66

10. Jen used 6 cookie sheets. She baked 14 cookies on each sheet. How many cookies did Jen bake?

²14
X 6
84

Unit Tests

Pull out and grade the class's unit exams covering multiplication, greater/lesser, and logical reasoning. Record the scores in your grade book. If you have more than four students, photocopy the exams.

Math Certificate

Honor your hardest-working math pupil with an award. Write the student's name on the certificate before presenting it to her.

CERTIFICATE ✦ ACHIEVEMENT
awarded to
Carrie Wise

MATH $MARTS!
Ms. Smart   October 19
Teacher   Date

19

Art

Spark your students' creativity with posters and crayons.

Coloring Poster

Pull out the poster to demonstrate art skills. As you help students color, show them how certain colors contrast with and complement each other and how dark and light colors can add dimension.

Crayons

Make a box of crayons for free-time coloring. Pull out the crayon box, fold, and glue or tape it on the side and bottom. Slip the "crayons" into the box before folding it closed.

Art Trophy

Recognize a star artist or the winner of an art show with a special trophy. To make one, glue small, painted wood pieces onto a round box lid. Pull out the "Artist Award" sticker to decorate the award.

Easel

Pull out the easel to display a different piece of art every day.

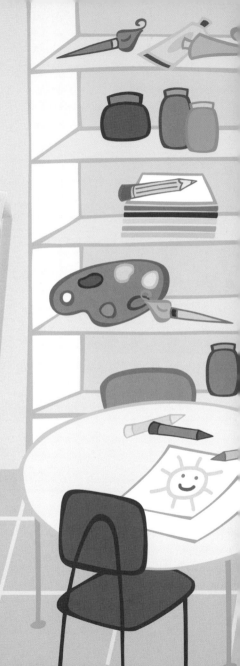

Music

Train budding musicians on a classroom piano.

Piano

Learning to play the piano can improve students' skills in other areas of school.

1. Fold 20-inch square of black paper in half from top down. Draw mark at 10 inches for middle. Fold in sides to meet at mark.

2. Open 1 flap, slip your fingers inside, and fold down top of flap to make triangle (like house with roof). Repeat on other side so that it looks like 2 houses side by side.

3. Fold center rectangle up to triangle bottoms. Fold rectangle up again so that bottom lines up with triangles.

4. Pull out piano keys. Fold in sides to stand piano upright. Cut out rectangle from back for doll's feet.

Sheet Music

Pull out the sheet music to "Mary Had a Little Lamb." Place it on the piano for beginning students to practice.

Bench

Cover a small round box with textured black paper.

Library Studies

Teach about the magic and information that can come from books.

Bookshelves

For library bookshelves, use the lid from a plastic bead box. Cover the back with paper if you like. Fill shelves with bitty books.

Books

Improve your school's library by gradually adding books. To make a starter collection, pull out the mini corrugated-cardboard pieces and the cover and spine stickers. Cover each book with colorful paper or leave it plain. Decorate with the stickers. Look for extra cardboard (or foam core) and stickers at craft stores to design even more books.

Library Cards

Give each student access to the library with her own card. Pull out the cards and fill in your students' names. If you have more than four students, photocopy the card.

Cookies

Kittens are Cute!

Public Library
Central, East, Downtown, Northwest & Ridgeway Branches

signature here

Lunch

Line up students alphabetically for a trip to the cafeteria.

Lunch Tray & Accessories

Lay a sheet of paper on a small rectangular plastic lid for a tray. Cut or punch out a small craft-foam circle for a plate. Fold a square of tissue paper in half for a napkin.

Lunch & Milk

Serve students a balanced lunch. For pretend sandwich bread, cut white foam-core board into small triangles, and glue on tan craft-foam edges for crust. Use craft foam for fillings. For an apple, cut a stem and leaf from craft foam, and glue them inside a red bead. Pull out the milk carton and fold it along the scored lines. Tape or glue the carton closed. Fold the top piece and glue it on the milk carton.

Lunch Tickets

Write students' names on the lunch tickets and pass them out. If you have more than four students, photocopy a ticket.

Lunch Ticket
School:
Issued to:
Date:
Amount:
signature here

Picture Day

Make a memento of your doll's school year.

Photo Tip Sheets

School photos are important keepsakes for parents, so make sure your students look their best on photo day. Review the tip sheet with the class the day before the photo shoot, or send a copy home with each student.

Photo Backgrounds

Nothing says "school photo" like traditional mottled backgrounds. Pull out the backgrounds, choose the color you prefer, and shoot your students in front of it. Snap!

Friends' School Photos

Students love sharing school photos. Pull out the school photos and pass them around.

PHOTO TIP SHEET

1. If students plan to use the photos for holiday cards, they should dress in holiday colors. If they want to pass them out or use the photos in scrapbooks, they should dress in costume or everyday wear.

2. Avoid white clothing. White can get dirty before a photo's taken, and it won't pop off the back~~ground~~ as other col~~ors~~

School Spirit

Encourage your students to let their spirit shine!

Spirit Patches

Create team wear for game days. Punch out the "Team AG" patch. Attach the patch to a white felt circle with double-stick tape. Draw "stitches" around the edge of the circle with a marker. Let dry, and then tape the patch onto a sporty shirt. If you have more than four students, photocopy the patch.

Shoe Flaps

Cut out crown-shaped flaps from white felt. Pull out the #1 circles and glue them to the flaps. Tape the flaps to the tops of sports shoes. If you have more than four students, photocopy the #1. Cut out the circles, and then glue them onto the felt flaps.

Go TEAM!

Stop to Share!

Send us your doll school ideas.

Write in cursive to:

Doll School **Editor**
American Girl
8400 Fairway Place
Middleton, WI 53562

(All comments and suggestions received by
American Girl may be used without compensation or
acknowledgment. Sorry—photos can't be returned.)

Here are some other American Girl books you might like:

❑ *I read it.*

❑ *I read it.*

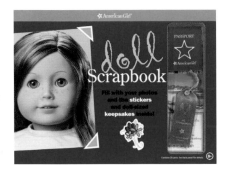

❑ *I read it.*

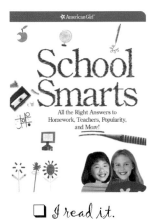

❑ *I read it.*